HYMN CLASSICS
FOR UKULELE

ISBN 978-1-5400-5755-6

Hal•Leonard®

Visit Hal Leonard Online at
www.halleonard.com

Contact us:
Hal Leonard
7777 West Bluemound Road
Milwaukee, WI 53213
Email: info@halleonard.com

In Europe, contact:
Hal Leonard Europe Limited
42 Wigmore Street
Marylebone, London, W1U 2RN
Email: info@halleonardeurope.com

In Australia, contact:
Hal Leonard Australia Pty. Ltd.
4 Lentara Court
Cheltenham, Victoria, 3192 Australia
Email: info@halleonard.com.au

All Creatures of Our God and King

Words by Francis of Assisi
Translated by William Henry Draper
Music from *Geistliche Kirchengesang*

First note

1. All crea - tures of our God and King, lift
2. Thou rush - ing wind that art so strong, ye
3.–6. *See additional lyrics*

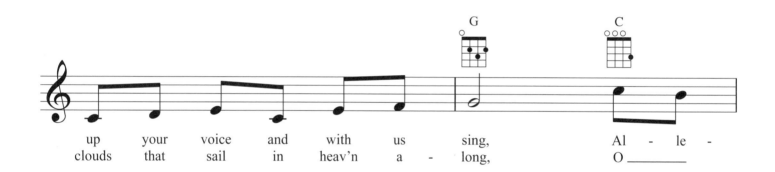

up your voice and with us sing, Al - le -
clouds that sail in heav'n a - long, O _____

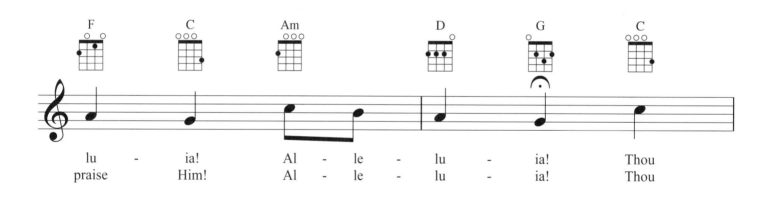

lu - ia! Al - le - lu - ia! Thou
praise Him! Al - le - lu - ia! Thou

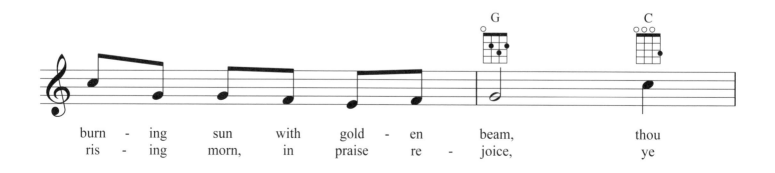

burn - ing sun with gold - en beam, thou
ris - ing morn, in praise re - joice, ye

sil - ver moon with soft - er gleam,
lights of eve - ning, find a voice!

O _____

Chorus

praise Him! O _____ praise Him! Al - le - lu - ia! Al - le -

lu - ia! Al - le - lu - ia!

Additional Lyrics

3. Thou flowing water, pure and clear,
Make music for thy Lord to hear,
Alleluia! Alleluia!
Thou fire so masterful and bright,
That givest man both warmth and light,
O praise Him! O praise Him!
Alleluia! Alleluia! Alleluia!

4. Dear mother earth, who day by day
Unfoldest blessings on our way,
O praise Him! Alleluia!
The flow'rs and fruits that in thee grow,
Let them His glory also show!
O praise Him! O praise Him!
Alleluia! Alleluia! Alleluia!

5. And all ye men of tender heart,
Forgiving others, take your part.
O sing ye! Alleluia!
Ye who long pain and sorrow bear,
Praise God and on Him cast your care!
O praise Him! O praise Him!
Alleluia! Alleluia! Alleluia!

6. Let all things their Creator bless,
And worship Him in humbleness.
O praise Him! Alleluia!
Praise, praise the Father, praise the Son,
And praise the Spirit, Three in One!
O praise Him! O praise Him!
Alleluia! Alleluia! Alleluia!

America, the Beautiful

Words by Katharine Lee Bates
Music by Samuel A. Ward

First note

Verse
Moderately

1. O beau - ti - ful for spa - cious skies, for am - ber waves of
2. O beau - ti - ful for pil - grim feet, whose stern, im - pas - sioned
3., 4. *See additional lyrics*

grain, for pur - ple moun - tain maj - es - ties a - bove the fruit - ed
stress, a thor - ough-fare for free - dom beat a - cross the wil - der -

Chorus

plain! A - mer - i - ca! A - mer - i - ca! God shed His grace on
ness! A - mer - i - ca! A - mer - i - ca! God mend thine ev - 'ry

thee, and crown thy good with broth - er-hood from sea to shin - ing sea.
flaw, con - firm thy soul in self - con-trol, thy lib - er - ty in law.

Additional Lyrics

3. O beautiful for heroes proved
   In liberating strife,
   Who more than self their country loved
   And mercy more than life!
   America! America!
   May God thy gold refine
   'Til all success be nobleness
   And every gain divine.

4. O beautiful for patriot dream
   That sees beyond the years;
   Thine alabaster cities gleam
   Undimmed by human tears.
   America! America!
   God shed His grace on thee,
   And crown thy good with brotherhood
   From sea to shining sea.

Beautiful Savior

Words from *Munsterisch Gesangbuch*
Translated by Joseph A. Seiss
Music adapted from Silesian Folk Tune

Battle Hymn of the Republic

Words by Julia Ward Howe
Music by William Steffe

First note

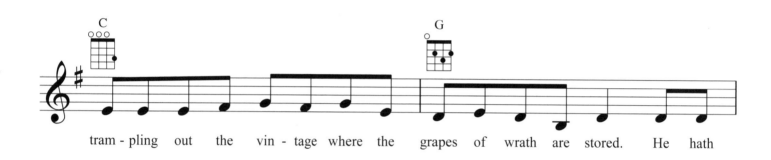

1. Mine eyes have seen the glo - ry of the com - ing of the Lord; He is
(2.–4.) *See additional lyrics*

tram - pling out the vin - tage where the grapes of wrath are stored. He hath

loosed the fate - ful light - ning of His ter - ri - ble swift sword; His

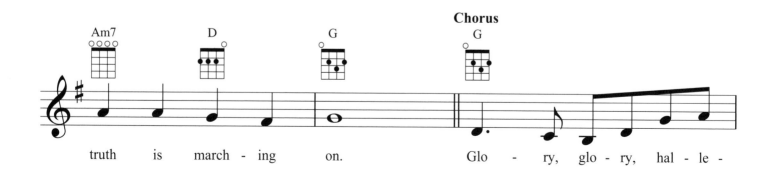

truth is march - ing on. Glo - ry, glo - ry, hal - le -

lu - jah! Glo - ry, glo - ry, hal - le - lu - jah.

Glo - ry, glo - ry, hal - le - lu - jah! His

truth is march - ing on.

2. I have on.
3. He has
4. In the

Additional Lyrics

2. I have seen Him in the watchfires of a hundred circling camps;
They have builded Him an altar in the evening dews and damps.
I can read His righteous sentence by the dim and flaring lamps;
His day is marching on.

3. He has sounded forth the trumpet that shall never sound retreat;
He is sifting out the hearts of men before His judgment seat.
O be swift, my soul, to answer Him! Be jubilant, my feet!
Our God is marching on.

4. In the beauty of the lilies Christ was born across the sea,
With a glory in His bosom that transfigures you and me.
As He died to make men holy, let us die to make men free,
While God is marching on.

Bringing in the Sheaves

Words by Knowles Shaw
Music by George A. Minor

1. Sow - ing in the morn - ing, sow - ing seeds of kind - ness,
2. Sow - ing in the sun - shine, sow - ing in the shad - ows;
3. Go - ing forth with weep - ing, sow - ing for the Mas - ter.

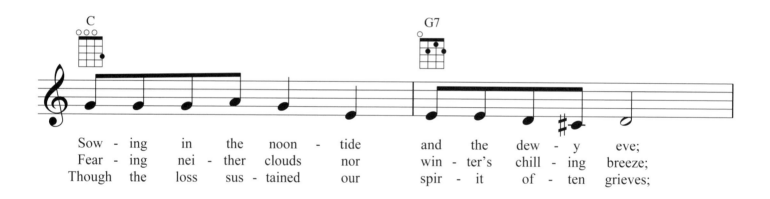

Sow - ing in the noon - tide and the dew - y eve;
Fear - ing nei - ther clouds nor win - ter's chill - ing breeze;
Though the loss sus - tained our spir - it of - ten grieves;

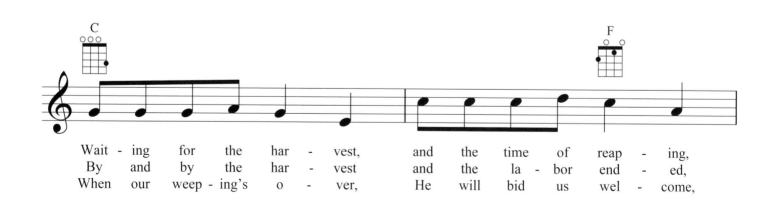

Wait - ing for the har - vest, and the time of reap - ing,
By and by the har - vest and the la - bor end - ed,
When our weep - ing's o - ver, He will bid us wel - come,

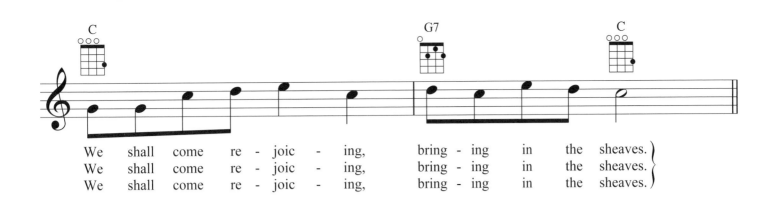

We shall come re - joic - ing, bring - ing in the sheaves.
We shall come re - joic - ing, bring - ing in the sheaves.
We shall come re - joic - ing, bring - ing in the sheaves.

Chorus

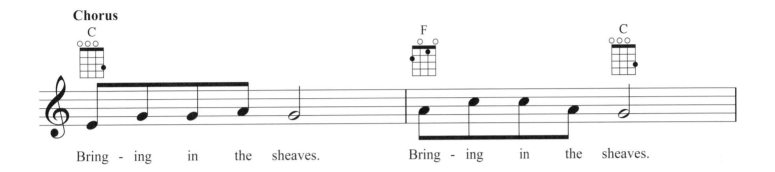

Bring - ing in the sheaves. Bring - ing in the sheaves.

We shall come re - joic - ing, bring - ing in the sheaves;

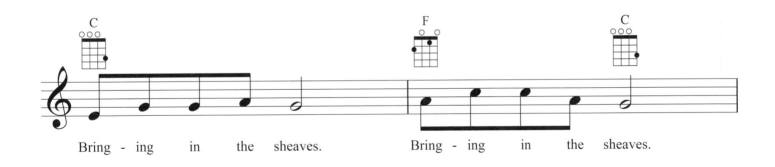

Bring - ing in the sheaves. Bring - ing in the sheaves.

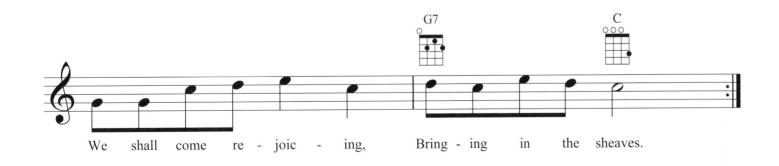

We shall come re - joic - ing, Bring - ing in the sheaves.

Christ the Lord Is Risen Today

Words by Charles Wesley
Music adapted from *Lyra Davidica*

Raise your joys and tri - umphs high,
Dy - ing once, He all doth save,
Death in vain for - bids Him rise,
Made like Him, like Him we rise,

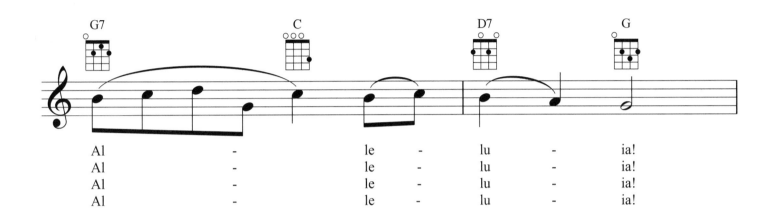

Al - le - lu - ia!
Al - le - lu - ia!
Al - le - lu - ia!
Al - le - lu - ia!

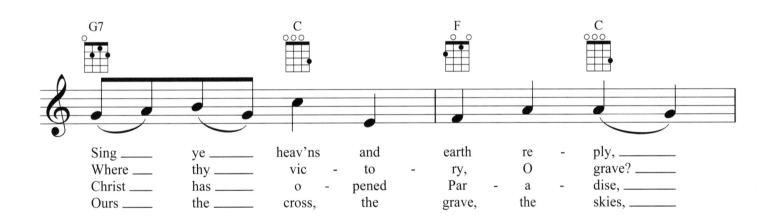

Sing ___ ye ___ heav'ns and earth re - ply, ___
Where ___ thy ___ vic - to - ry, O grave? ___
Christ ___ has ___ o - pened Par - a - dise, ___
Ours ___ the ___ cross, the grave, the skies, ___

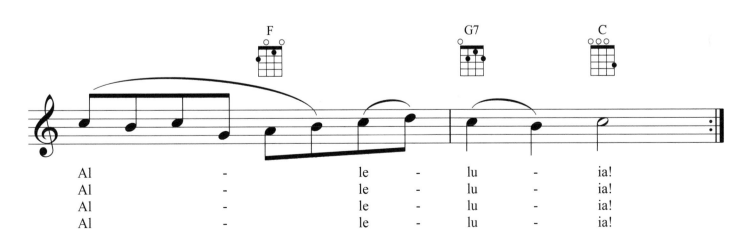

Al - le - lu - ia!
Al - le - lu - ia!
Al - le - lu - ia!
Al - le - lu - ia!

The Church's One Foundation

Words by Samuel John Stone
Music by Samuel Sebastian Wesley

First note

Verse
Stately

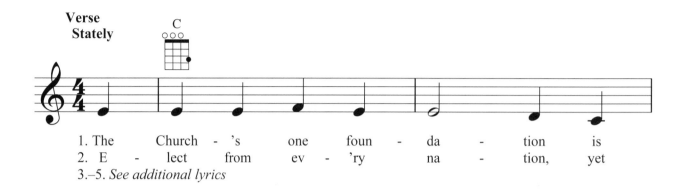

1. The Church - 's one foun - da - tion is
2. E - lect from ev - 'ry na - tion, yet

3.–5. *See additional lyrics*

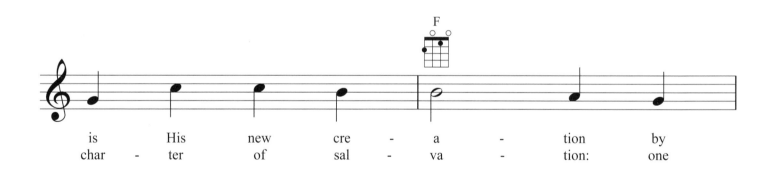

Je - sus Christ her Lord. She
one o'er all the earth, Her

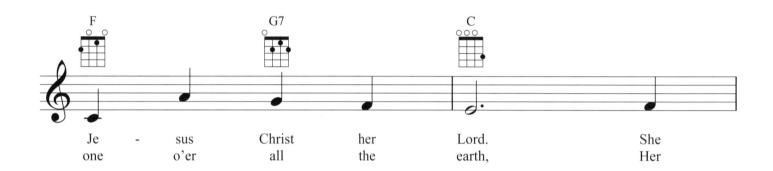

is His new cre - a - tion by
char - ter of sal - va - tion: by one

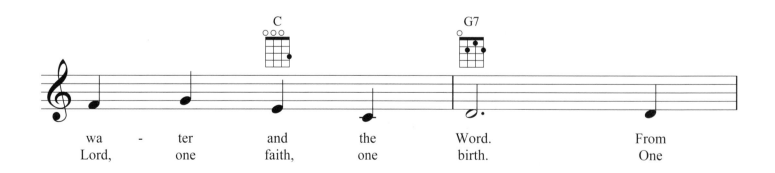

wa - ter and the Word. From
Lord, one faith, one birth. One

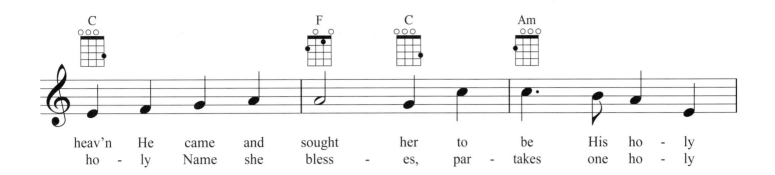

heav'n He came and sought her to be His ho - ly
ho - ly Name she bless - es, par - takes one ho - ly

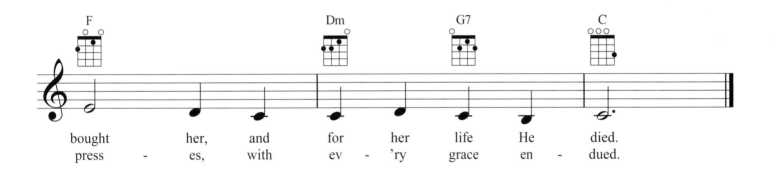

bride. With His own blood he
food, and to one hope she

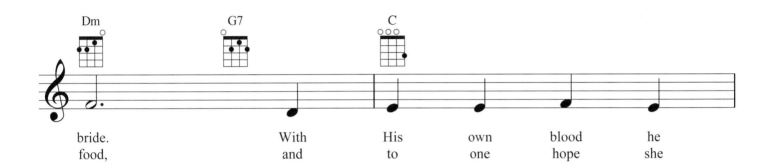

bought her, and for her life He died.
press - es, with ev - 'ry grace en - dued.

Additional Lyrics

3. Though with a scornful wonder men see her sore oppressed,
   By schisms rent asunder, by heresies distressed;
   Yet saints their watch are keeping, their cry goes up, "How long?"
   And soon the night of weeping shall be the morn of song.

4. 'Mid toil and tribulation and tumult of her war,
   She waits the consummation of peace forevermore;
   Till with the vision glorious her longing eyes are blessed,
   And the great Church victorious shall be the Church at rest.

5. Yet she on earth hath union with God, the Three in One,
   And mystic sweet communion with those whose rest is won.
   O happy ones and holy! Lord, give us grace that we,
   Like them, the meek and lowly, on high may dwell with Thee.

Come, Thou Almighty King

Traditional
Music by Felice de Giardini

Faith of Our Fathers

Words by Frederick William Faber
Music by Henri F. Hemy and James G. Walton

1. Faith of our fa - thers, liv - ing still,
2. Faith of our fa - thers, we ___ will strive
3. Faith of our fa - thers, we ___ will love

in spite of dun - geon, fire ___ and sword;   O how our hearts ___ beat
to win all na - tions un - to thee;   and through the truth ___ that
both friend and foe in all ___ our strife;   and preach thee, too, ___ all

high ___ with joy   when - e'er we hear that glo - rious word!
comes ___ from God,   man - kind shall then be tru - ly free.
love ___ knows how,   by kind - ly words and vir - tuous life.

Chorus

Faith of our fa - thers, ho - ly faith!

We will be true to thee till death.

God of Grace and God of Glory

Words by Harry Emerson Fosdick
Music by John Hughes

First note

Verse
Stately

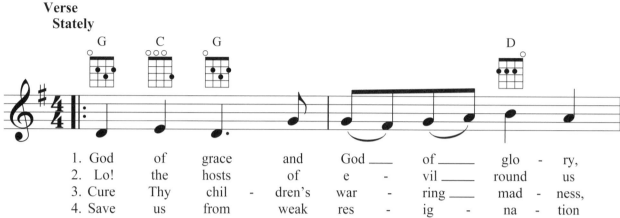

1. God of grace and God ____ of ____ glo - ry,
2. Lo! the hosts of e - vil ____ round us
3. Cure Thy chil - dren's war - ring ____ mad - ness,
4. Save us from weak res - ig - na - tion

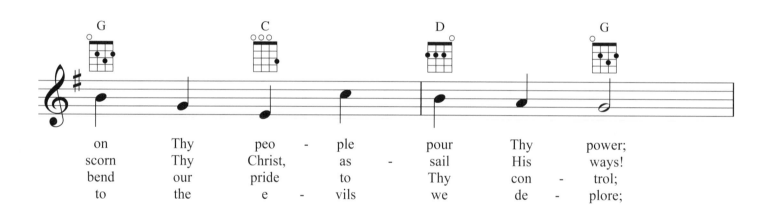

on Thy peo - ple pour Thy power;
scorn Thy Christ, as - sail His ways!
bend our pride to Thy con - trol;
to the e - vils we de - plore;

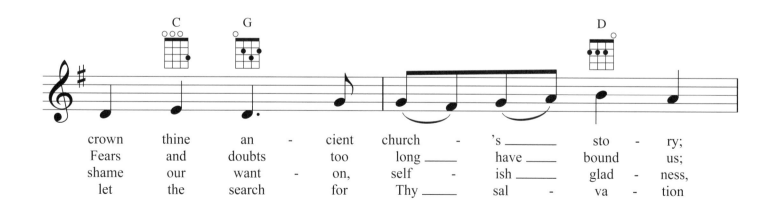

crown thine an - cient church - 's ____ sto - ry;
Fears and doubts too long ____ have ____ bound us;
shame our want - on, self - ish ____ glad - ness,
let the search for Thy ____ sal - va - tion

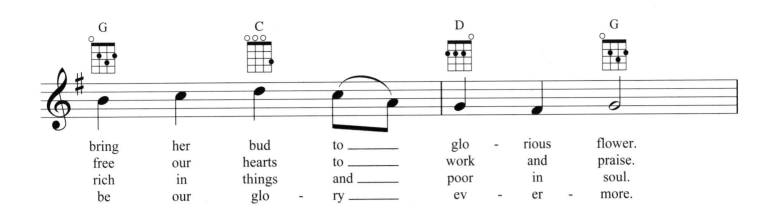

G	C		D	G

bring her bud to _____ glo - rious flower.
free our hearts to _____ work and praise.
rich in things and _____ poor in soul.
be our glo - ry _____ ev - er - more.

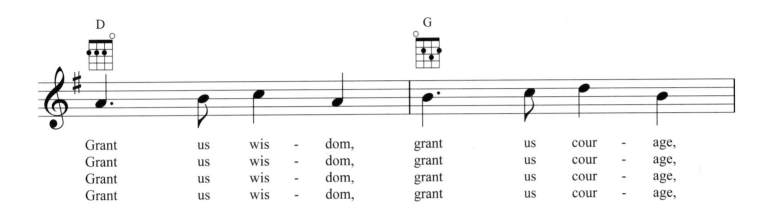

D	G

Grant us wis - dom, grant us cour - age,
Grant us wis - dom, grant us cour - age,
Grant us wis - dom, grant us cour - age,
Grant us wis - dom, grant us cour - age,

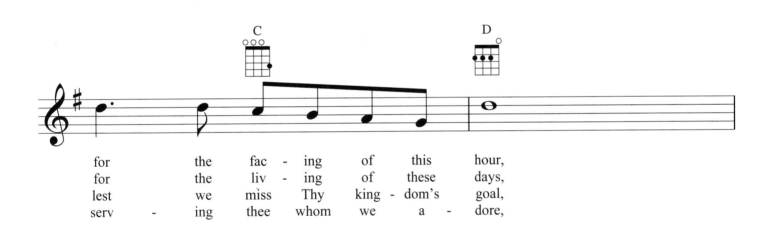

C	D

for the fac - ing of this hour,
for the liv - ing of these days,
lest we miss Thy king - dom's goal,
serv - ing thee whom we a - dore,

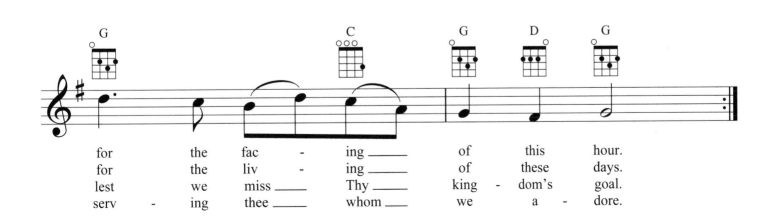

G	C	G	D	G

for the fac - ing _____ of this hour.
for the liv - ing _____ of these days.
lest we miss _____ Thy _____ king - dom's goal.
serv - ing thee _____ whom _____ we a - dore.

Great Is Thy Faithfulness

Words by Thomas O. Chisholm
Music by William M. Runyan

Have Thine Own Way, Lord

Words by Adelaide A. Pollard
Music by George C. Stebbins

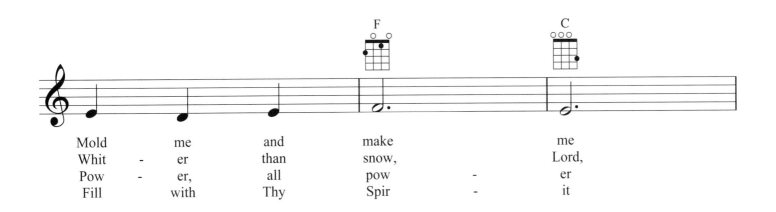

Mold me and make me me
Whit - er than snow, Lord,
Pow - er, all pow - er
Fill with Thy Spir - it

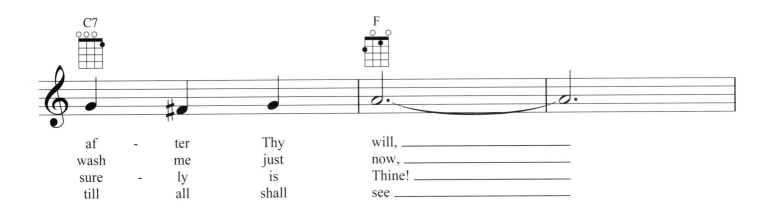

af - ter Thy will, _____
wash me just now, _____
sure - ly is Thine! _____
till all shall see _____

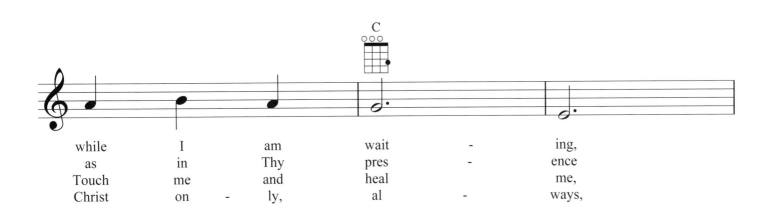

while I am wait - ing,
as in Thy pres - ence
Touch me and heal me,
Christ on - ly, al - ways,

Yield - ed and still. _____
Hum - bly I bow. _____
Sav - ior di - vine. _____
Liv - ing in me! _____

I Love to Tell the Story

Words by A. Catherine Hankey
Music by William G. Fischer

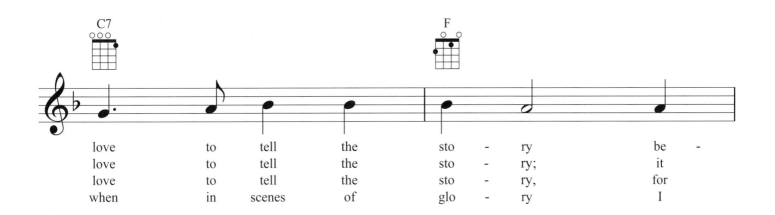

love	to	tell	the	sto	-	ry	be	-
love	to	tell	the	sto	-	ry;	it	
love	to	tell	the	sto	-	ry,	for	
when	in	scenes	of	glo	-	ry	I	

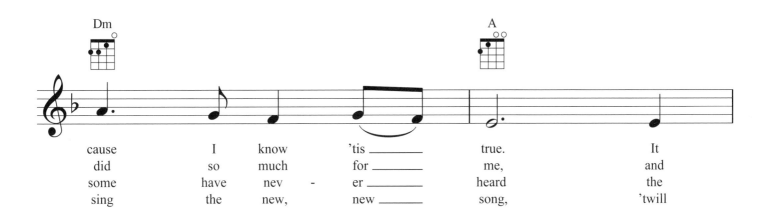

cause	I	know	'tis _____	true.	It
did	so	much	for _____	me,	and
some	have	nev - er _____	heard	the
sing	the	new,	new _____	song,	'twill

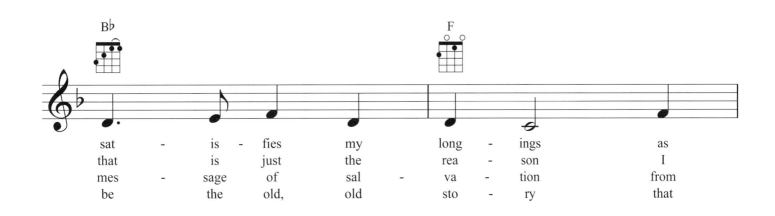

sat	-	is	fies	my	long	-	ings	as
that	is	just	the	rea	-	son	I	
mes	-	sage	of	sal	-	va	-	tion	from
be	the	old,	old	sto	-	ry	that	

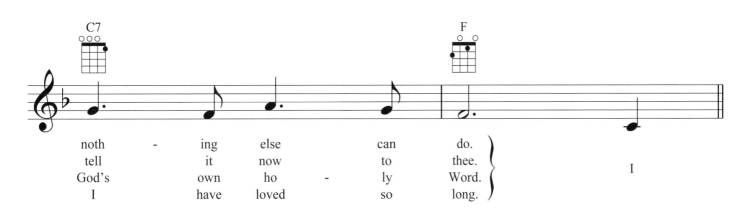

noth	-	ing	else	can	do.	
tell	it	now	to	thee.	}	
God's	own	ho	-	ly	Word.	}	I
I	have	loved	so	long.	}	

Chorus

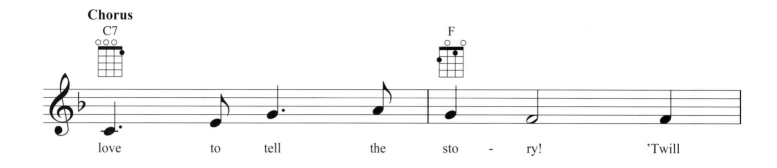

love to tell the sto - ry! 'Twill

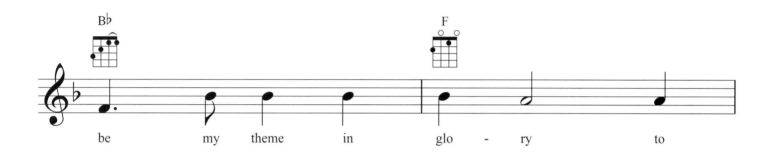

be my theme in glo - ry to

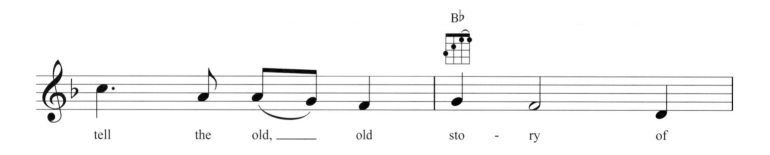

tell the old, _____ old sto - ry of

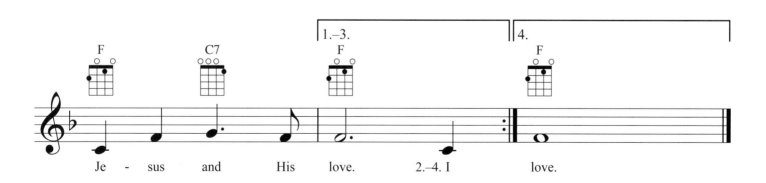

Je - sus and His love. 2.–4. I love.

Immortal, Invisible

Words by Walter Chalmers Smith
Traditional Welsh Melody
from John Roberts' *Canaidau y Cyssegr*

1. Im - mor - tal, in - vis - i - ble, God on - ly wise, in
2.–4. *See additional lyrics*

light in - ac - ces - si - ble hid from our eyes. Most

bless - ed, most glo - rious, the An - cient of Days; Al -

might - y, vic - to - rious, Thy great name we praise.

Additional Lyrics

2. Unresting, unhasting, and silent as light,
Nor wanting, not wasting, Thou rulest in might.
Thy justice like mountains high soaring above
Thy clouds, which are fountains of goodness and love.

3. To all life Thou givest, to both great and small;
In all life Thou livest, the true life of all.
We blossom and flourish as leaves on the tree,
And wither and perish, but naught changeth Thee.

3. Great Father of glory, pure Father of light,
Thine angels adore Thee, all veiling their sight.
All praise we would render; O help us to see,
'Tis only the splendor of light hideth Thee.

I Sing the Mighty Power of God

Words by Isaac Watts
Music from *Gesangbuch der Herzogl*

First note

Verse
Majestically

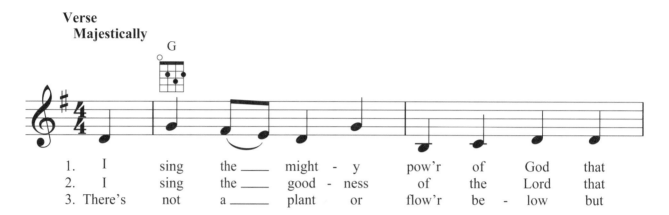

1. I sing the ____ might - y pow'r of God that
2. I sing the ____ good - ness of the God Lord that
3. There's not a ____ plant or flow'r be - low but

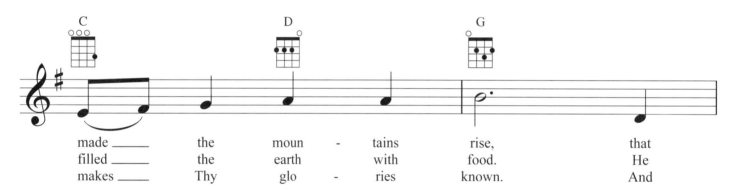

made ____ the moun - tains rise, that
filled ____ the earth with food. He
makes ____ Thy glo - ries known. And

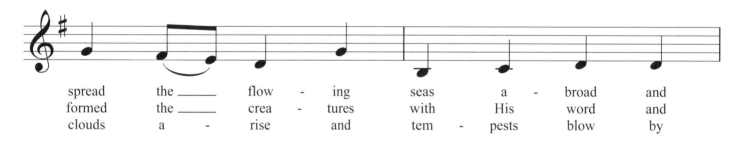

spread the ____ flow - ing seas a - broad and
formed the ____ crea - tures with His word and
clouds a - rise and tem - pests blow by

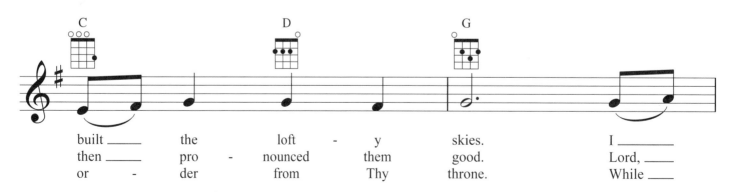

built ____ the loft - y skies. I ____
then ____ pro - nounced them good. Lord, ____
or - der from Thy throne. While ____

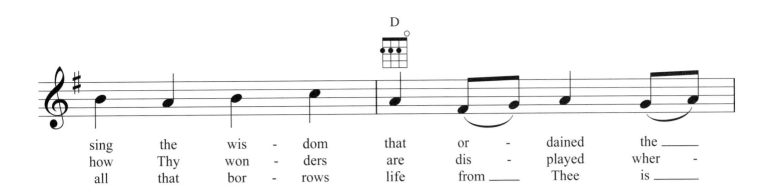

sing the wis - dom that or - dained the _____
how Thy won - ders that are dis - played wher -
all that bor - rows life from ____ Thee is _____

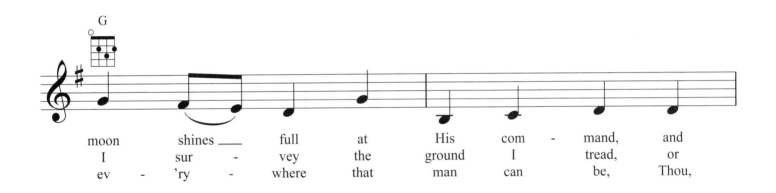

sun to rule the day. The
e'er I turn in my eye, if
ev - er in Thy care, and

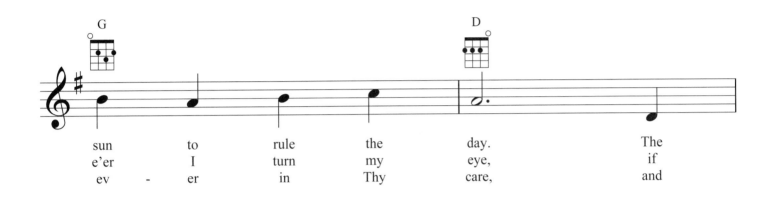

moon shines ____ full at His com - mand, and
I sur - vey at the ground I tread, or
ev - 'ry - where that man can be, Thou,

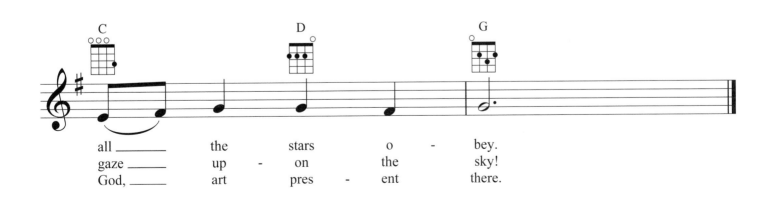

all _____ the stars o - bey.
gaze _____ up - on the sky!
God, _____ art pres - ent there.

I Stand Amazed in the Presence
(My Savior's Love)
Words and Music by Charles H. Gabriel

First note

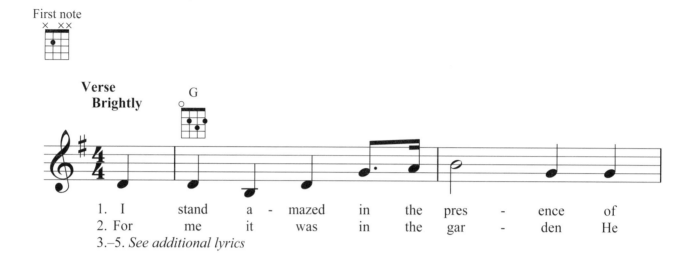

Verse
Brightly

1. I stand a - mazed in the pres - ence of
2. For me it was in the gar - den He
3.–5. *See additional lyrics*

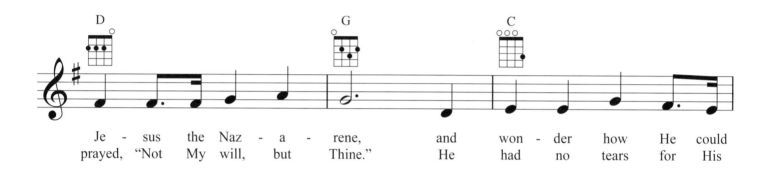

Je - sus the Naz - a - rene, and won - der how He could
prayed, "Not My will, but Thine." He had no tears for His

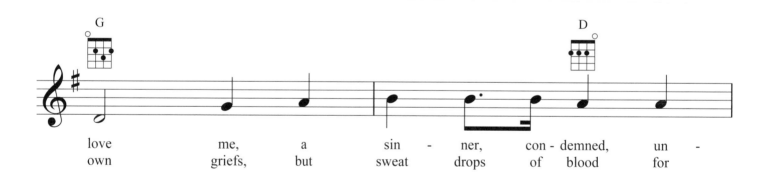

love me, a sin - ner, con - demned, un -
own griefs, but sweat drops of blood for

Chorus

clean. }
mine. } How mar - vel - ous! How won - der - ful!

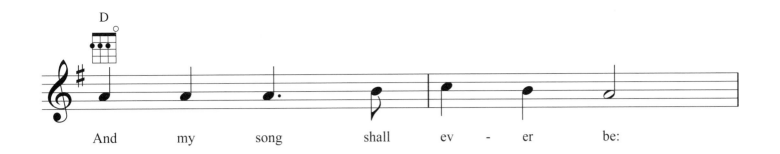

And my song shall ev - er be:

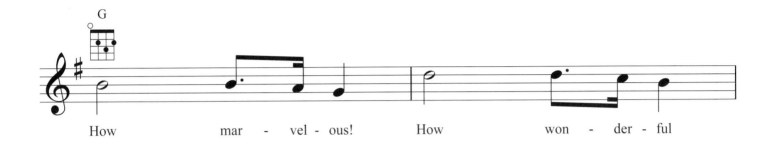

How mar - vel - ous! How won - der - ful

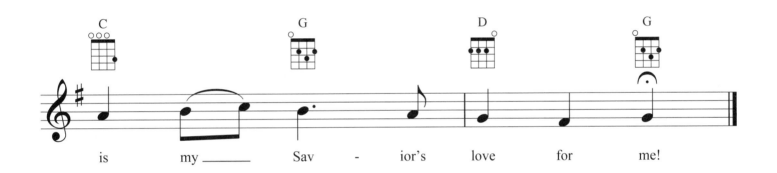

is my _____ Sav - ior's love for me!

Additional Lyrics

3. In pity angels beheld Him,
   And came from the world of light
   To comfort Him in the sorrows
   He bore for my soul that night.

4. He took my sins and my sorrows,
   He made them His very own.
   He bore the burden to Calv'ry
   And suffered and died alone.

5. When with the ransomed in glory
   His face I at last shall see,
   'Twill be my joy through the ages
   To sing of His love for me.

Jesus, Keep Me Near the Cross

Words by Fanny J. Crosby
Music by William H. Doane

First note

Verse
Moderately

1. Je - sus, keep me near the cross, there a pre - cious foun - tain,
2. Near the cross, a trem - bling soul, love and mer - cy found me;
3. Near the cross! O Lamb of God, bring its scenes be - fore me;
4. Near the cross I'll watch and wait, hop - ing, trust - ing ev - er,

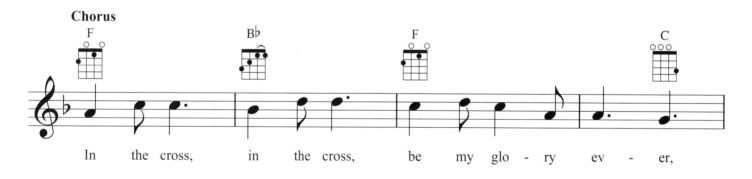

free to all, a heal - ing stream, flows from Cal - v'ry's moun - tain.
there the Bright and Morn - ing Star sheds its beams a - round me.
help my walk from day to day with its shad - ows o'er me.
till I reach the gold - en strand just be - yond the riv - er.

Chorus

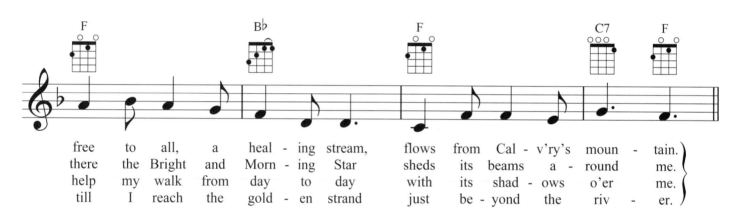

In the cross, in the cross, be my glo - ry ev - er,

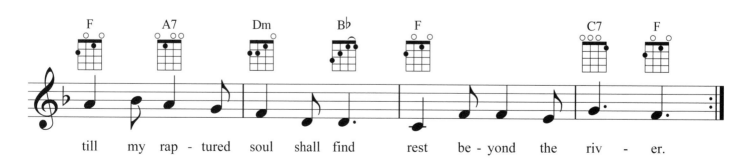

till my rap - tured soul shall find rest be - yond the riv - er.

Jesus Loves Me

Words by Anna B. Warner
Music by William B. Bradbury

First note

1. Je - sus loves me; this I know, for the Bi - ble tells me so.
2.–4. *See additional lyrics*

Lit - tle ones to Him be - long; they are weak, but He is strong.

Chorus

Yes, Je - sus loves me! Yes, Je - sus loves me!

Yes, Je - sus loves me; the Bi - ble tells me so.

Additional Lyrics

2. Jesus loves me; He who died,
   Heaven's gates to open wide.
   He will wash away my sin,
   Let His little child come in.

3. Jesus loves me; loves me still,
   Though I'm very weak and ill.
   From His shining throne on high,
   Comes to watch me where I lie.

4. Jesus loves me; He will stay
   Close beside me all the way.
   If I love Him, when I die,
   He will take me home on high.

Lead On, O King Eternal

Words by Ernest W. Shurtleff
Music by Henry T. Smart

1. Lead on, O King E - ter - nal, The day of march has
2. Lead on, O king E - ter - nal, Till sin's fierce war shall
3. Lead on, O King E - ter - nal, We fol - low, not with

come; Hence - forth in fields of con - quest Thy tents shall be our
cease, And ho - li - ness shall whis - per The sweet A - men of
fears; For glad - ness breaks like morn - ing Wher - e'er Thy face ap -

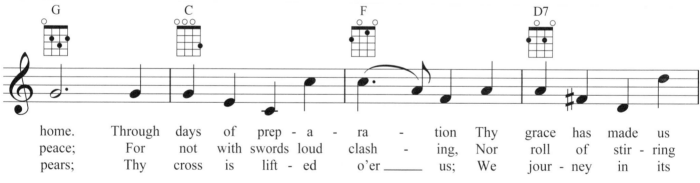

home. Through days of prep - a - ra - tion Thy grace has made us
peace; For not with swords loud clash - ing, Nor roll of stir - ring
pears; Thy cross is lift - ed o'er _____ us; We jour - ney in its

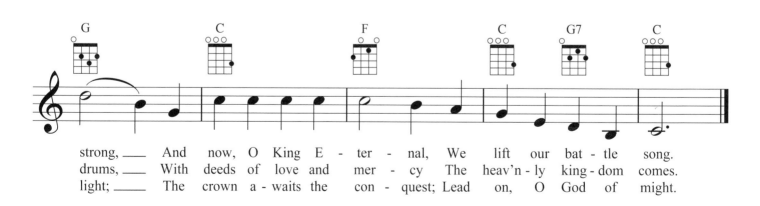

strong, ____ And now, O King E - ter - nal, We lift our bat - tle song.
drums, ____ With deeds of love and mer - cy The heav'n - ly king - dom comes.
light; ____ The crown a - waits the con - quest; Lead on, O God of might.

Praise to the Lord, the Almighty

Words by Joachim Neander
Translated by Catherine Winkworth
Music from *Erneuerten Gesangbuch*

Rock of Ages

Words by Augustus M. Toplady
v.1,2 altered by Thomas Cotterill
Music by Thomas Hastings

First note

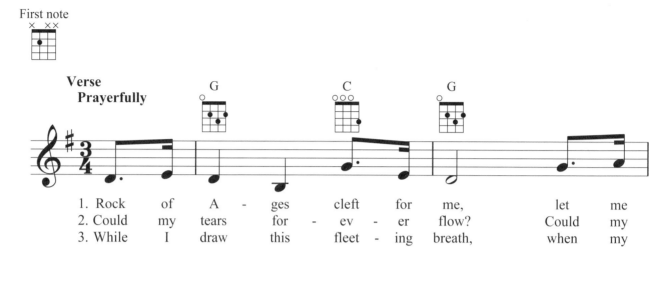

1. Rock of A - ges cleft for me, let me
2. Could my tears for - ev - er flow? Could my
3. While I draw this fleet - ing breath, When my

hide my - self in Thee. Let the wa - ter and the
zeal no lan - guor know? These for sin could not a -
eyes shall close in death, when I rise to worlds un -

blood, from Thy wound - ed side which flowed, be of
tone, Thou must save and Thou a - lone. In my
known, and be - hold Thee on Thy throne, Rock of

sin the dou - ble cure; save from wrath and make me pure.
hand no price I bring; sim - ply to Thy cross I cling.
A - ges cleft for me, let me hide my - self in Thee.

Stand Up, Stand Up for Jesus

Words by George Duffield, Jr.
Music by George J. Webb

First note

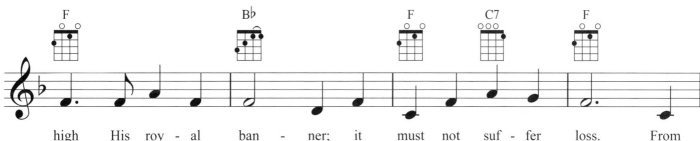

1. Stand up, stand up for Je - sus, ye sol - diers of the cross. Lift
2. Stand up, stand up for Je - sus, the trum - pet call o - bey. Forth
3. Stand up, stand up for Je - sus, stand in His strength a - lone. The
4. Stand up, stand up for Je - sus, the strife will not be long. This

high His roy - al ban - ner; it must not suf - fer loss. From
to the might - y con - flict in this His glo - rious day. Ye
arm of flesh will fail you; ye dare not trust your own. Put
day the noise of bat - tle; the next, the vic - tor's song. To

vic - t'ry un - to vic - t'ry His ar - my shall He lead, _____ till
that are men, now serve Him a - gainst un - num - bered foes. _____ Let
on the gos - pel ar - mor, each piece put on with prayers. ___ Where
him who o - ver - com - eth a crown of life shall be; _____ He

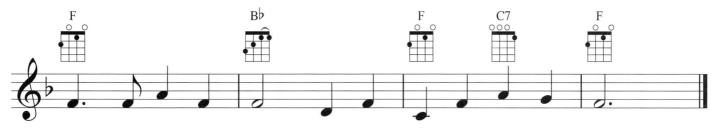

ev - 'ry foe is van - quished and Christ is Lord in - deed.
cour - age rise with dan - ger, and strength to strength op - pose.
du - ty calls, or dan - ger, be nev - er want - ing there.
with the King of glo - ry shall reign e - ter - nal - ly.

Softly and Tenderly

Words and Music by Will L. Thompson

1. Soft - ly and ten - der - ly Je - sus is call - ing,
2. Why should we tar - ry when Je - sus is plead - ing,
3. Time is now fleet - ing, the mo - ments are pass - ing,
4. O, for the won - der - ful love He has prom - ised,

call - ing for you and for me.
plead - ing for you and for me?
pass - ing from you and from me.
prom - ised for you and for me!

See, on the por - tals He's wait - ing and watch - ing,
Why should we lin - ger and heed not His mer - cies,
Shad - ows are gath - er - ing, death's night is com - ing,
Though we have sinned, He has mer - cy and par - don,

watch - ing for you and for me. _____
mer - cies for you and for me? _____
com - ing for you and for me. _____
par - don for you and for me. _____

Come

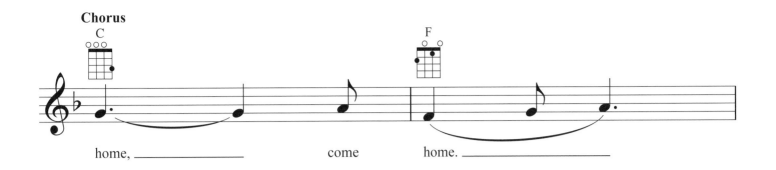

home, _____ come home. _____

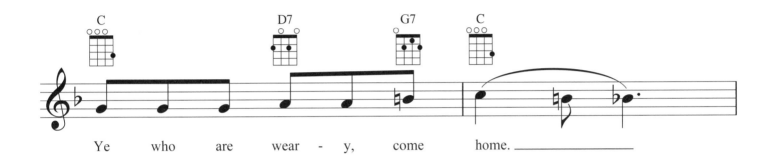

Ye who are wear - y, come home. _____

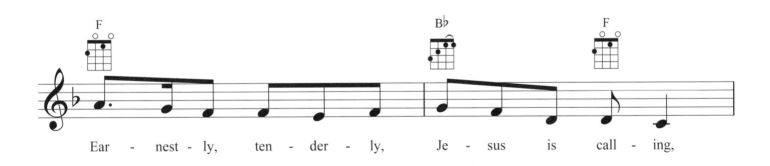

Ear - nest - ly, ten - der - ly, Je - sus is call - ing,

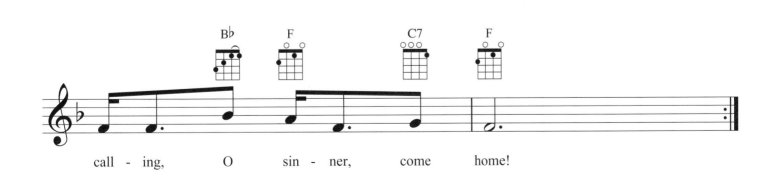

call - ing, O sin - ner, come home!

Sweet Hour of Prayer

Words by William W. Walford
Music by William B. Bradbury

First note

Verse
Gently

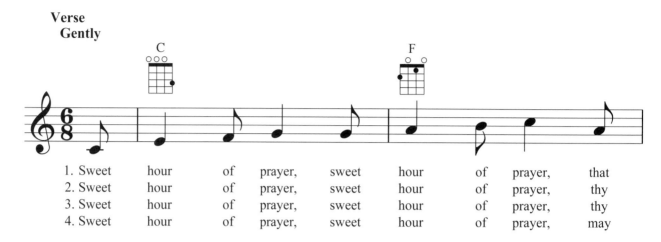

1. Sweet   hour   of   prayer,   sweet   hour   of   prayer,   that
2. Sweet   hour   of   prayer,   sweet   hour   of   prayer,   thy
3. Sweet   hour   of   prayer,   sweet   hour   of   prayer,   thy
4. Sweet   hour   of   prayer,   sweet   hour   of   prayer,   may

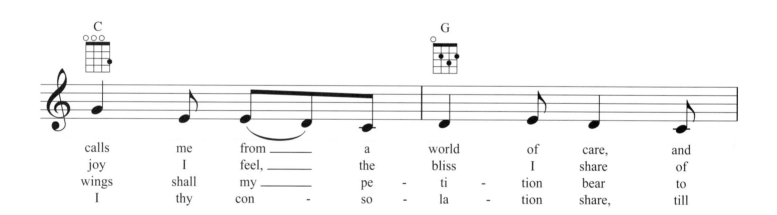

calls   me   from   a   world   of   care,   and
joy   I   feel,   the   world   bliss   I   share   of
wings   shall   my   pe - ti - tion   bear   to
I   thy   con - so - la - tion   share,   till

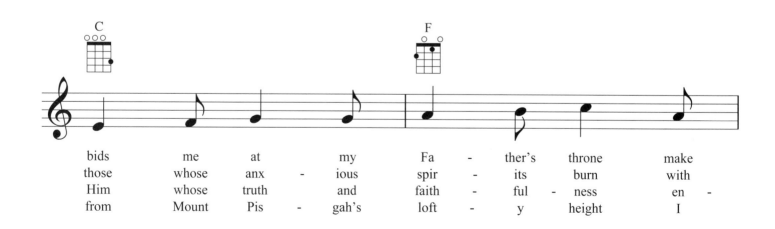

bids   me   at   my   Fa - ther's   throne   make
those   whose   anx - ious   spir - its   burn   with
Him   whose   truth   and   faith - ful - ness   en -
from   Mount   Pis - gah's   loft - y   height   I

We Gather Together

Words from *Nederlandtsch Gedenckclanck*
Translated by Theodore Baker
Netherlands Folk Melody
Arranged by Edward Kremser

First note

Flowing

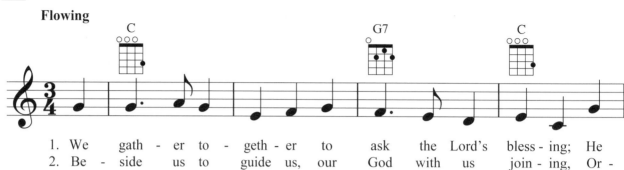

1. We gath-er to-geth-er to ask the Lord's bless-ing; He
2. Be-side us to guide us, our God with us join-ing, Or-
3. We all do ex-tol Thee, Thou Lead-er tri-um-phant, And

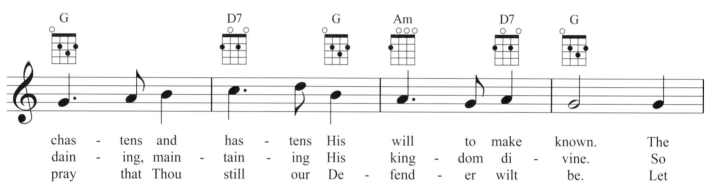

chas-tens and has-tens His will to make known. The
dain-ing, main-tain-ing His king-dom di-vine. So
pray that Thou still our De-fend-er wilt be. Let

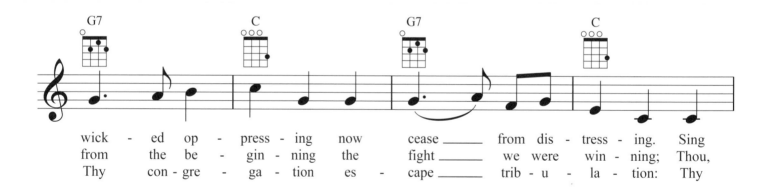

wick-ed op-press-ing now cease ____ from dis-tress-ing. Sing
from the be-gin-ning the fight ____ we were win-ning; Thou,
Thy con-gre-ga-tion es-cape ____ trib-u-la-tion: Thy

prais-es to His name ____ He for-gets not His own.
Lord, wast at our side, ____ all ____ glo-ry be Thine!
name be ev-er praised! ____ O ____ Lord, make us free!